Flower-and-Bird

Painting in Ancient China

Flower-and-Bird
Painting in Ancient China

CHINA INTERCONTINENTAL PRESS

Preface

The Chinese ancestors who invented the original pictographic Chinese characters also developed, with the passage of time, the unique traditional Chinese painting, which falls into three genres: flower-and-bird, landscape and figure drawing.

The flower-and-bird painting traces its history back to ancient times. It embraced many different schools and a large number of accomplished painters came to the fore. Archaeological data show that in the Neolithic Age, people already used "brushes" and natural pigments to draw flowers, birds and fish on pottery, which can be regarded as the embryo of China's flower-and-bird painting. Abstract birds and animals were engraved on bronze ware of the Shang (1600–1046 BC) and Zhou (1046–256 BC) dynasties.

Archaeologists also found phoenixes drawn on silk belonging to the Warring States Period (475–221 BC) and *zhuque* (similar to phoenix, referring to the seven southern mansions of the 28 lunar mansions in ancient astronomy) on silk and lacquer ware of the Western Han Dynasty (206 BC–AD 25). As late as the Eastern Han Dynasty (25–220) appeared relatively mature flower-and-bird paintings.

According to historical materials, during the Wei Kingdom (220–265), Jin Dynasty (265–420), Northern and Southern Dynasties (386–589) some painters began to specialize in flower-and-bird painting, marking that divorced from figure and landscape drawing, it entered Chinese art as an independent genre. The Tang

Dynasty (618–907) was a period in which the new genre reached maturity. With their technique being perfected day by day, more professional painters were expert at drawing flowers and birds. Both the Five Dynasties (907–960) and the Yuan Dynasty (1206–1368) saw further improvement of flower-and-bird painting, which entered its heyday actually in the sandwiched Song Dynasty (960–1279). The two dynasties of Ming (1368–1644) and Qing (1616–1911) produced numerous flower-and-bird masters, making the genre known to the Western world.

Those painters depicted a great variety of subjects, including flowers, plants, birds, beasts, vegetables, fruits, mountain rocks, and fish, to express their feelings and understanding of nature. In this way, flower-and-bird painting can be rated as a perfect combination of traditional Chinese culture and art.

Many subjects, known very well by the public, have commonly accepted implications. For instance, the peony stands for wealth and rank, orchid for elegance, lotus for self-preservation and moral integrity, chrysanthemum for honor in one's later years, plum for innate pride and iron determination, bamboo for tenacity and indomitableness, pomegranate for fertility, pine and crane for longevity, mandarin ducks for love, fish for abundance, and so on.

These exquisite paintings are highly aesthetic, with many being kept by private collectors and museums at home and abroad. Some have become China's national treasures.

The technique of drawing ranges from *gong-bi* (fine, delicate brushwork), *xie-yi* (freehand brushwork) to the combination of the two. The paintings are mainly drawn on silk or paper in the form of horizontal scroll, vertically-hung scroll, album and fan. In terms of the use of color, there are five methods: colored painting, line-drawing, *shui-mo* painting (ink and wash), *po-mo* painting (splash-ink), and *mo-gu* or "boneless" painting (drawing without outline but with forms achieved by washes of ink and color). Many drawing skills like *shui-mo*, *po-mo* and *mo-gu* were created distinctively by Chinese painters, making flower-and-bird painting a unique art-form in the world.

China's traditional flower-and-bird

painting and Western painting have both similarities and differences.

Classical Western still-life painting gives priority to accurately reproducing an object's original shape. In other words, a sense of visual accuracy is prerequisite to judging a painter's skill and understanding his or her aesthetic conception.

The works of Chinese painters cover a relatively wider range of subjects. They paid more attention to the creation of *yi-jing* (artistic mood). Therefore, they sought after similarity in spirit rather than formal resemblance, and underscored the integrity and harmony of a tableau. As a result, the viewers can often feel a particular charm and appeal from these paintings.

Table of Contents

Flower-and-bird Paintings of the Five Dynasties and the Two Song Dynasties

20	Dan Feng You Lu Tu (Red Maples and Crying Deer)	Painter unknown
21	Sui Zhao Tu (New Year's First Day)	Zhao Chang
22	Shan Zhe Ji Que Tu (Partridges, Brambles and Sparrows)	Huang Jucai
24	Jia He Cao Chong Tu (Good Paddy Crops, Weeds and Insects)	Wu Bing
25	Mu Xue Han Qin Tu (Evening Snow and Winter Bird)	Ma Lin
26	Mo Zhu Tu (Inked Bamboo)	Wen Tong
27	Zi Mu Ji Tu (Mother Hen and Her Chicks)	Painter unknown
28	Wu Se Ying Wu Tu (Colorful Parrot)	Zhao Ji
29	La Mei Shan Qin Tu (Wintersweet and Tits)	Zhao Ji
30	Liu Ya Lu Yan Tu (Crows on a Willow Tree and Wild Geese in Reed Marshes)	Zhao Ji
32	Zhu Que Tu (Sparrows in a Bamboo Grove)	Zhu Rui
34	Pi Pa Kong Que (Loquat and Peacocks)	Cui Bai

36   Han Que Tu (Winter Sparrows)   Cui Bai

38   Fu Gui Hua Li Tu (Peonies and a Cat)   Painter unknown

40   Cui Zhu Ling Mao Tu (Green Bamboos and Birds)   Painter unknown

41   Xue Lu Shuang Yan (Two Wild Geese in the Snow-clad Reeds)   Painter unknown

42   Xue Shu Han Qin Tu (Winter Bird Perching on a Snow-clad Tree)   Li Di

44   Yang Liu Ru Que Tu (Young Sparrows on a Willow Branch)   Painter unknown

45   Ping Po Shan Niao Tu (Titmouse on an Apple Branch)   Painter unknown

46   Li Zhi Bo Zhao Tu (Shrikes)   Painter unknown

47   Ji Xiang Duo Zi Tu (Auspiciousness and Fertility)   Lu Zonggui

48   Yu Lan Lou Qin Tu Tuan Shan (Fan Painting of Magnolia and Bird)   Painter unknown

49   Hai Tang Tu (Flowering Crab-apple)   Lin Chun

Flower-and-bird Paintings of the Yuan Dynasty

52   Hua Niao (Flowers and Birds)   Bian Lusheng

54   Lu Yan (Wild Geese in Reeds)   Lin Liang

56   Ku He Xi Chi (Withered Lotus and Water Birds)   Zhang Zhong

58   Qiu Ye Shuang Qin Tu (Autumn Leaves and Two Birds)   Painter unknown

59   Jiu Que Xian Chun Tu (A Turtledove Heralding the Advent of Spring)   Painter unknown

60   Jia Shang Ying Tu (A Hawk on a Stand)   Allegedly by Xu Ze

61   Yu Zao Tu (Fish and Algae)   Painter unknown

62   Ku Mu Zhu Shi Tu (Withered Trees, Bamboos and Rocks)   Zhao Mengfu

63   Mo Mei Tu (Inked Plum Flowers)   Wang Mian

64   Zhu Shi Ji Qin Tu (Bamboos, Rocks and Gathering Birds)   Wang Yuan

66   Zhu Shi Tu (Bamboos and Rocks)   Painter unknown

68   Tao Zhu Yuan Yang Tu (Peach Trees, Bamboos and Mandarin Ducks)   Painter unknown

Flower-and-bird Paintings of the Ming Dynasty

72   San You Bai Qin Tu ('Three Friends' and 100 Birds)   Bian Wenjin

74   Chun Hua San Xi (Spring Blossom and Three Magpies)   Bian Wenjin

76   Hua Niao (Flowers and Birds)   Zhou Zhimian

78   Li Shi Cong Hui Tu (Upright Rocks and Flowers in Clusters)   Tang Yin

79   Shu Cai (Vegetable)   Shen Zhou

80   Jiu Sheng Huan Yu (Turtledove Calling for Rain)   Shen Zhou

81   Shui Xian La Mei (Narcissuses and Wintersweet)   Qiu Ying

82   Lan Zhu Tu (Orchid and Bamboo)   Wen Zhengming

84   Hua Hui Cao Chong Tu (Flowers, Plants and Insects)   Chen Hongshou

86   She Se Hua Hui (Colored Flowers)   Chen Chun

88   Qiu Lu Fu Rong (Autumn Egrets and Hibiscus)   Lü Ji

90   Song Niao Tu (Pine and Birds)   Wang Zhong

92   Xian He (Crane)   Zhang Pingshan

94   Hua Niao Tu (A Flower-and-bird Painting)   Zhang Chong

Flower-and-bird Paintings of the Qing Dynasty

100   Hua Hui (Flowers)   Yun Shouping

102   Mo Gu Hua Hui Tu Ce (An Imitation of An Ancient Flower Album-I)   Yun Shouping

103   Mo Gu Hua Hui Tu Ce (An Imitation of An Ancient Flower Album-II)   Yun Shouping

104   Mo Gu Hua Hui Tu Ce (An Imitation of An Ancient Flower Album-III)   Yun Shouping

105   Ying Su Tu (Poppy Flowers)   Liu Yu

106   Ju Hua Tu (Chrysanthemums)   Lang Shih-ning

107   Shao Yao Tu (Herbaceous Peony Flowers)   Lang Shih-ning

108   Yu Mei Ren Hu Die Hua Tu (Corn Poppy and Fringed Iris)   Lang Shih-ning

109   Gu Hua Ji Sui Tu (Millet Flowers and Spikes)   Lang Shih-ning

110   Jin Chun Tu (Spring Pheasants)   Lang Shih-ning

112   Wu Tong Shuang Tu (Phoenix Tree and a Pair of Rabbits)   Leng Mei

114   Mu Dan Shuang Shou Tu (Peony Flowers and a Pair of Paradise Flycatchers)   Yu Xing

116   Fu Rong Xi Shui Tu (Waterside Hibiscus Flowers)   Li Bingde

117   He Hua Tu (Lotus Flowers)   Li Bingde

118   Xie Sheng Shu Guo Tu (A Sketch of Vegetables)   Yuan Jiang

119	Xue Jiao Shuang He Tu (Snow-clad Banana Tree and a Pair of Cranes)	Yuan Yao
120	He Hua Tu (Lotus Flowers)	Liu Shu
121	Yu Tang Fu Gui Tu (Wealth and Honor)	Yu Yuan
122	San Ba Tu (Offering Birthday Felicitations)	Zhao Zhiqian
123	Song He Yan Nian (Pine Tree and Cranes for Longevity)	Li Shan
124	Hua Hui Tu Ce (Album of Flowers-I)	Xiang Shengmo
125	Hua Hui Tu Ce (Album of Flowers-II)	Xiang Shengmo
126	Hua Hui Tu (Flowers-I)	Zhao Zhiqian
127	Hua Hui Tu (Flowers-II)	Zhao Zhiqian
128	Gui Hua (Sweet-scented Osmanthus)	Jiang Tingxi
130	Hua Guo Tu (Flowers and Fruits-I)	Zhou Xian
131	Hua Guo Tu (Flowers and Fruits-II)	Zhou Xian
132	Hua Hui (Flowers)	Wang Wu
133	Hua Niao (Flowers and Birds)	Wang Wu

134	Ju (Chrysanthemums)	Yun Bing
135	Hua Hui (Flowers)	Cixi
136	Shu Guo (Vegetables and Fruits)	Lu Hui
137	Qiu Hua Qi Shi Tu (Autumn Flowers and Rock)	Shen Shijie
138	Hua Niao Tu (Flowers and Birds-I)	Ren Xun
139	Hua Niao Tu (Flowers and Birds-II)	Ren Xun
140	Hua Niao Tu (Flowers and Birds-I)	Ren Yi
141	Hua Niao Tu (Flowers and Birds-II)	Ren Yi
142	Hua Hui (Flowers)	Ma Jiatong
144	Shu Hua He Bi Tu (A Combination of Calligraphy and Painting-I)	Wu Changshuo
145	Shu Hua He Bi Tu (A Combination of Calligraphy and Painting-II)	Wu Changshuo

Flower-and-bird Paintings of the Five Dynasties

and the Two Song Dynasties

Very few flower-and-bird paintings made before the 10th century have been handed down to this very day.

Flower-and-bird painting entered into a stage of great innovation and rapid development during the Five Dynasties (907-960) with the technique of drawing gradually attaining to perfection. Meanwhile, various schools with distinctive styles and features appeared. One was represented by Huang Quan (903−965), another by Xu Xi (937−975).

Huang had served as an imperial painter for many years. Drawing materials from exotic flowers and herbs, rare birds and animals that were planted and raised in the imperial gardens and palaces, his paintings were characterized by meticulous depiction and bright colors, and acclaimed as *Huang jia fu gui* (the Huang school's characteristic magnificence).

Though coming from a prominent family, Xu had never entered into officialdom. Actually, either flowers, plants, vegetables, fruits and insects in gardens or water birds and fish in brooks were worthy of his brush. His paintings full of idyllic taste thus produced a fresh artistic conception, and his style was called *Xu Xi ye yi* (Xu Xi's unconventional, original charm).

The two schools have had an immense influence upon flower-and-bird painting of later ages. The drawing technique of Huang Quan was inherited by his sons Huang Jucai (933−?) and Huang Jubao (whose dates of birth and death are unknown), and developed into the well-known "Huang Style." Xu Xi's followers included his grandsons Xu Chongsi and Xu Chongju, who were both famous flower-and-bird painters in the Northern Song Dynasty (960−1127).

China's flower-and-bird painting enjoyed its first heyday in the Northern and Southern Song dynasties, during which the practice of establishing an Imperial Art Academy in the Five Dynasties was still in use. Following in the footsteps of their Five Dynasties predecessors, painters of the Northern Song Dynasty paid more attention to sketching, with their brushwork becoming finer and smoother. The championship and participation of Emperor

Huizong (1082−1135) further boosted the creation of flower-and-bird painting. Artists of the entire country gathered in the imperial palace, and scored unprecedented successes. The imperial-court decorative painting featuring delicate, exquisite strokes gradually attained to maturity; and what's more, both freehand brushwork painting and literati painting began to come to the fore at that time. The former portrays objects in ink and wash with succinct, bold strokes, and produces an effect of running ink by means of the *Xuan* paper (high-quality rice paper made in east China's Anhui Province); while the latter themed withered trees, bamboos, rocks, orchids and plums expresses the temperament and taste of literary scholars, which is very different from what's seen in the works of imperial and folk artists.

Besides those living through the Five Dynasties and the Northern Song Dynasty like Huang Jucai, Huang Jubao, Xu Chongsi and Xu Chongju, important flower-and-bird painters of this period (the two Song dynasties) included Zhao Chang, Wu Bing, Ma Lin, Wen Tong, Emperor Huizong, Cui Bai, Bian Luan, Li Di, Yang Wujiu, Zhao Mengjian and Liang Kai. Their profound influence can be traced in the works of later artists.

**Dan Feng You Lu Tu
(Red Maples and Crying Deer)
Painter unknown
Five Dynasties (10th century)
Color on silk
64.6 × 118.5cm**

Vividly depicting a group of deer
in a maple grove just after the
autumn frost, the artist uses
the colors directly without first
making sketches to produce
an effect of running ink.

Sui Zhao Tu
(New Year's First Day)
Zhao Chang
Northern Song Dynasty
(960—1127)
Color on silk
103.8 × 51.2cm

Zhao Chang is a painter living in the early stage of the Northern Song Dynasty. The dates of his birth and death are unknown. Zhao is well versed in drawing flowers, plants and insects in bright colors. Styling himself "Sketcher Zhao Chang," he won great renown in his lifetime. This is his representative work.

Shan Zhe Ji Que Tu
(Partridges,Bram bles and Sparrows)
Huang Jucai
Northern Song Dynasty (960−1127)
Color on silk
53.6 × 97cm

This work of art had been kept in the
imperial palace of the Qing Dynasty.
Delineating mountain rocks, brambles
and birds with simple strokes, it
sparkles with wit and humor.

Jia He Cao Chong Tu
(Good Paddy Crops, Weeds and Insects)
Wu Bing
SouthernSong Dynasty (1127—1279)
Ink and wash on paper
58 × 40cm

Wu Bing is an imperial painter of the Southern Song Dynasty. The dates of his birth and death are unknown. This sketch displays the artist's superb skill.

Mu Xue Han Qin Tu
(Evening Snow and Winter Bird)
Ma Lin
Southern Song Dynasty (1127—1279)
Ink and wash on paper
58 × 40cm

Ma Lin, son of painter Ma Yuan, is a famous artist of the Southern Song Dynasty. He is expert in drawing portraits, landscape, flowers and birds. The snowy scene depicted in this picture is permeated with a desolate atmosphere.

Mo Zhu Tu (Inked Bamboo)
Wen Tong
Northern Song Dynasty (960–1127)
Ink and wash on silk
104.4 × 130.1cm

Wen Tong (1018-1079) is a well-known flower-and-bird painter of the Northern Song Dynasty. He is good at painting bamboos in ink. His drawing technique has made a notable impact on later artists.

Zi Mu Ji Tu (Mother Hen and Her Chicks)
Painter unknown
Song Dynasty (960–1279)
Color on paper
32.8 × 60.8cm

This picture had been a collected article in the imperial palace of the Qing Dynasty.

Wu Se Ying Wu Tu (Colorful Parrot)
Zhao Ji
Northern Song Dynasty (960–1127)
Color on silk
53.3 × 125.1cm

Zhao Ji is the name of Emperor Huizong (1082–1135). A celebrated painter and calligrapher, he is good at sketching and flower-and-bird drawing. His works are noted for rich colors and energetic vitality.

**La Mei Shan Qin Tu
(Wintersweet and Tits)
Zhao Ji
Northern Song Dynasty (960–1127)
Color on silk
82.8 × 52.8cm**

The picture depicts a couple of birds snuggling together on a wintersweet tree that breaks out into blossom in the severe winter.

山禽矜逸態
梅粉弄輕柔
已有丹青約
千秋指白頭

宣和殿御製并書

Liu Ya Lu Yan Tu
(Crows on a Willow Tree and Wild Geese in Reed Marshes)
Zhao Ji
Northern Song Dynasty (960–1127)
Color on paper
34 × 223cm

Once kept in the imperial palace of the Qing Dynasty, this piece of artwork is
Emperor Huizong's representative work.

Zhu Que Tu
(Sparrows in a Bamboo Grove)
Zhu Rui
Northern Song Dynasty (960–1127)
Color on paper
158 × 65cm

An imperial painter of the Northern
Song Dynasty, Zhu Rui is expert in
drawing landscape, flowers and birds.
The dates of his birth and death are
unknown. This picture shows birds, all
different in form, twittering in a dense
grove of bamboos. One feels as if he
could almost hear what they're singing.

Pi Pa Kong Que
(Loquat and Peacocks)
Cui Bai
Northern Song Dynasty (960—1127)
Color on silk
183.1 × 109.8cm

Cui Bai (1024—1068), a member of
the Imperial Art Academy of the
Northern Song Dynasty, is good at
character sketching and flower-and-
bird drawing. This picture, one of his
representative works, had been a
precious collection of the royal
storehouse of the Song, Ming and
Qing dynasties.

Han Que Tu (Winter Sparrows)
Cui Bai
Northern Song Dynasty (960–1127)
Color on silk
25.5 × 101.4cm

Also a collection of the Qing imperial palace, compared with "Pi Pa Kong Que," this picture is permeated with a melancholy atmosphere but full of wild appeal.

寒雀争寒宅
枝如栱且枒
妬設有鴶
末飲捨簪
苧敫護
壬午春日

**Fu Gui Hua Li Tu
(Peonies and a Cat)
Painter unknown
Song Dynasty (960–
1279)
Color on silk
140 × 107.5cm**

The painter portrays
a spotted cat and
several peonies that
stand for wealth and
rank with vivid,
delicate brushwork.

Cui Zhu Ling Mao Tu
(Green Bamboos and Birds)
Painter unknown
Song Dynasty (960–1279)
Color on silk
185 × 109.9cm

In a graphic and realistic way, the
painter delineates bamboos,
rocks, pheasants and birds with
fine, meticulous strokes.

Xue Lu Shuang Yan (Two Wild Geese in the Snow-clad Reeds)
Painter unknown
Song Dynasty (960–1279)
Color on silk
174.6 × 99.5cm

With feeling and setting happily blended, this piece of artwork reflects the tradition of valuing sketch training by the painters of the Song Dynasty.

Xue Shu Han Qin Tu (Winter Bird Perching on a Snow-clad Tree)
Li Di
Southern Song Dynasty (1127—1279)
Color on silk
116.1 × 53cm

The picture presents a bleak and chilly winter scene. Li Di is particularly versed in classical Chinese paintings featuring birds and animals. The dates of his birth and death are unknown.

43

Yang Liu Ru Que Tu
(Young Sparrows on a Willow Branch)
Painter unknown
Song Dynasty (960-1279)
24.8 × 24.8cm

This picture, vividly depicting several nestlings on a willow branch, is the work of a master hand.

**Ping Po Shan Niao Tu
(Titmouse on an Apple Branch)
Painter unknown
Song Dynasty (960-1279)
24.8 × 24.8cm**

This picture depicting a titmouse standing on an apple branch is of classic beauty and in elegant taste.

Li Zhi Bo Zhao Tu (Shrikes)
Painter unknown
Song Dynasty(960-1279)
Color on silk
40 × 40cm

The Song Dynasty painters are good at sketching from nature, and their extant flower-and-bird, vegetable-and-fruit, and figure paintings all demonstrate consummate skill. This picture depicting a couple of shrikes is the work of a master hand.

Ji Xiang Duo Zi Tu (Auspiciousness and Fertility)
Lu Zonggui
Southern Song Dynasty (1127—1279)
Color on silk
24 × 25.8cm

Lu Zonggui of the Southern Song Dynasty is skilled in painting flowers, bamboos, birds and animals, and particularly noted for his sketches. Both the pomegranate and loquat fruits in this picture stand for fertility.

Yu Lan Lou Qin Tu Tuan Shan
(Fan Painting of Magnolia and Bird)
Painter unknown
Southern Song Dynasty (1127–1279)
Color on silk
23.2 × 24.8cm

The composition of this drawing made with fine, accurate strokes is ingeniously conceived.

Hai Tang Tu (Flowering Crab-apple)
Lin Chun
Southern Song Dynasty (1127-1279)
Color on silk
40 × 40cm

A disciple of painter Zhao Chang, Lin Chun from Qiantang (the present Hangzhou, Zhejiang Province) is noted for his rigorous, meticulous style and good at sketching from nature. This picture is drawn in splendid colors.

Flower-and-bird Paintings of the Yuan Dynasty

Following the Five Dynasties (907—960) and the two Song dynasties (960—1279), the Yuan Dynasty (1206—1368) saw new development in the creation of flower-and-bird paintings. Observing the doctrine of "back to the ancients," some influential painters living through the Song and Yuan dynasties like Zhao Mengfu and Qian Xuan stressed the importance of imitating ancient masters, while advocating the application of calligraphic skill to painting and the expression of personal taste.

The literati painting rising from the Song Dynasty scored considerable achievements during the Yuan Dynasty. Like their predecessors of the Song Dynasty, literati painters at this time also favored the subject matters of plum, orchid, bamboo and chrysanthemum, and were particularly skilled in drawing withered trees, mountain rocks, inked bamboos and inked plums. They painted mountains and trees to vent personal feelings and convey their thoughts and aspirations. Under their brushes, priority had been given to similarity in spirit rather than formal resemblance, and creating a lofty artistic ambience had become a common pursuit. Leading painters included Ke Jiusi, Ni Zan, Wu Zhen and Wang Mian, and quite a number of their works like "Inked Bamboos" by Ke Jiusi, "Withered Trees, Bamboos and Rocks" by Zhao Mengfu and "Inked Plums" by Wang Mian were known far and wide.

Technically, literati painters of the Yuan Dynasty employed various drawing skills at the same time, combining *gong-bi* (fine, delicate brushwork) with *xie-yi* (freehand brushwork), *shui-mo* (ink and wash) with *bai-miao* (line drawing), and the technique of *po-mo* (splash-ink) was being perfected daily in practice, which laid a foundation for the prosperity of flower-and-bird painting in the following Ming Dynasty (1368—1644).

The influence of the thriving literati painting could be also traced in the works of imperial painters who, while continuing to obey the tradition of being meticulous, realistic and magnificent, turned to use simple strokes to produce a tranquil, elegant artistic conception.

Renowned flower-and-bird painters of the Yuan Dynasty also included Bian Lusheng and Zhang Zhong who were both widely imitated in later periods.

Hua Niao (Flowers and Birds)
Bian Lusheng
Yuan Dynasty (1206−1368)
Color on silk
120 × 55cm

Bian Lusheng of the Yuan Dynasty is expert in wash painting of flowers and birds. The dates of his birth and death are unknown, and not many of his works have been handed down to today.

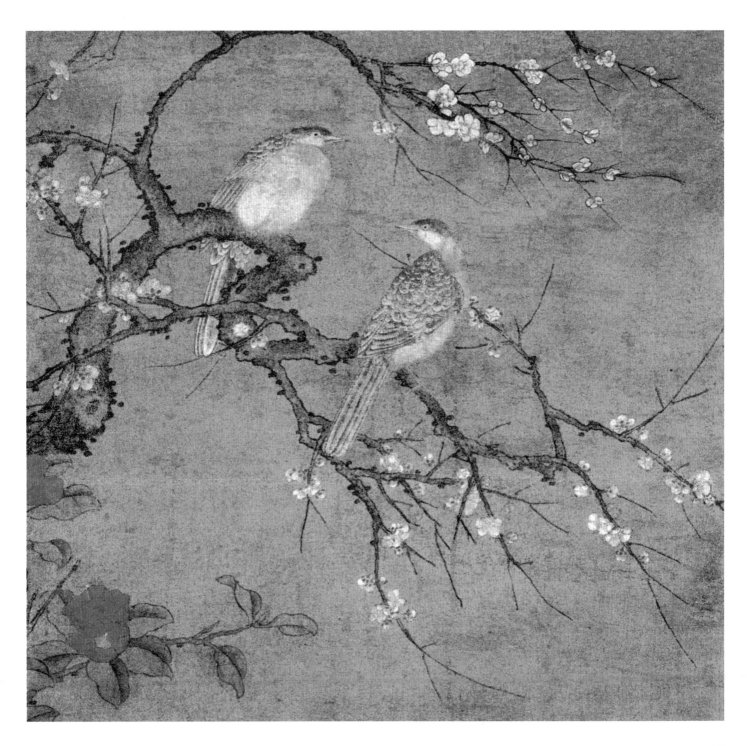

Lu Yan (Wild Geese in Reeds)
Lin Liang
Yuan Dynasty (1206−1368)
Color on paper
161 × 84cm

Lin Liang (1436−1487) is a representative figure of the imperial-court painters in the middle period of the Ming Dynasty. Good at drawing flowers and birds, he portrays a wide range of subjects. In this picture he depicts wild geese in ink and wash with roughly freehand brushwork, while drawing flowers and plants in a meticulous way, which is his typical style.

Ku He Xi Chi (Withered Lotus and Water Birds)
Zhang Zhong
Yuan Dynasty (1206–1368)
Color on paper
96.4 × 46cm

Zhang Zhong (1335–1368) of the Yuan Dynasty is well versed in portraying flowers, birds, bamboos and mountain rocks with simple, unconventional brushwork. Viewers can thus find a flavor of literati painting from his works. This picture characterized by both delicate and freehand brushwork is a most smooth and vigorous piece of artwork, and had been collected by the royal storehouse of the Qing Dynasty.

Qiu Ye Shuang Qin Tu
(Autumn Leaves and Two Birds)
Painter unknown
Yuan Dynasty (1206—1368)
Color on silk
22.8 × 22.6cm

It was allegedly drawn by Ma Lin (the 13th century). A couple of birds perching on a twig lends some joy of life to the bleak and chilly late autumn scene as depicted in this picture with simple composition.

**Jiu Que Xian Chun Tu
(A Turtledove Heralding the
Advent of Spring)
Painter unknown
Yuan Dynasty (1206–1368)
Color on paper
150.9 × 31.3cm**

The painter portrays
camellias, bamboos and a
flying bird in rich, harmonious
colors with the technique of
shuang-gou (first making
sketches and then filling the
contour with ink).

**Jia Shang Ying Tu
(A Hawk on a Stand)
Allegedly by Xu Ze
Yuan Dynasty (1206−1368)
Color on silk
54.2 × 98.1cm**

It is reportedly drawn by Xu Ze of
the Yuan Dynasty. Xu portrays
the very life-like hawk in rich,
bright colors with delicate
strokes, fully displaying his
refined skill. The dates of Xu's
birth and death are unknown.

Yu Zao Tu (Fish and Algae)
Painter unknown
Yuan Dynasty (1206—1368)
Color on paper
141.9 × 59.6cm

The painter portrays three fish, duckweeds and algae with vivid, accurate touches.

弄墨如子經意神常超
能金錯刀松雪篆中何
作石無非作飛白法作竹藁

Ku Mu Zhu Shi Tu (Withered Trees, Bamboos and Rocks)
Zhao Mengfu
Yuan Dynasty (1206—1368)
Ink and wash on paper
763.5 × 32.9cm

Zhao Mengfu (1254—1322) is a renowned, very influential calligrapher and painter of the Yuan Dynasty, especially good at drawing characters, horses, landscape and flowers. As a calligrapher, both his *kai-shu* (regular script) and *xing-shu* (running script) are reportedly matchless. Zhao creates a fresh, elegant artistic ambience in this scroll with a strong flavor of literati painting.

Mo Mei Tu (Inked Plum Flowers)
Wang Mian
Yuan Dynasty (1206—1368)
Ink and wash on paper
90.3 × 27.6cm

Wang Mian (1287—1359) is a well-known poet and painter of the Yuan Dynasty, especially good at drawing inked plums, bamboos and mountain rocks. The plum he drew with luxuriant foliage and spreading blossoming branches has a peculiar charm and distinctive features of its own.

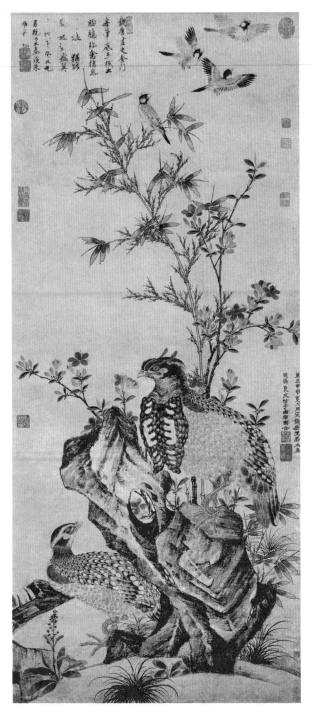

Zhu Shi Ji Qin Tu (Bamboos, Rocks and Gathering Birds)
Wang Yuan
Yuan Dynasty (1206–1368)
Ink and wash on paper
137.7 × 59.6cm

Wang Yuan is a famous painter of the Yuan Dynasty. The dates of his birth and death are unknown. Once under the tutelage of Zhao Mengfu, Wang is good at character sketching and landscape drawing, and his inked flower-and-bird paintings are known far and wide.

Zhu Shi Tu
(Bamboos and Rocks)
Painter unknown
Yuan Dynasty (1206−1368)
Ink and wash on paper
58 × 40cm

This picture with simple
composition presents a
bleak and desolate sight of
withered trees, bamboos
and mountain rocks.

Tao Zhu Yuan Yang Tu (Peach Trees, Bamboos and Mandarin Ducks)
Painter unknown
Yuan Dynasty (1206—1368)
Color on silk
176.2 × 109.5cm

It was allegedly drawn by Wang Yuan of the Yuan Dynasty. Peach trees in full bloom, lush and green bamboos, chirping bird on a branch, mandarin ducks playing on water -- much is expressed in the limited space of this picture scroll.

Flower-and-bird Paintings of the Ming Dynasty

The Ming Dynasty (1368−1644) is an important period serving as a link between past and future in the history of China's flower-and-bird painting. Artists of this time championed the doctrine of "back to the ancients," received their training under different masters, and formed various schools. These included the Wu School (mainly composed of painters living in Suzhou and the nearby area with Shen Zhou as the representative figure), the Four Master Painters (namely Shen Zhou, Wen Zhengming, Tang Yin and Qiu Ying who lived in the middle stage of the Ming Dynasty. In their works they produced a tranquil and peaceful atmosphere, aiming at expressing the cultivated pleasures of a leisurely life), the so-called "Southern Chen and Northern Cui" (namely Chen Hongshou and Cui Zizhong), the Huating School (named after Huating, the hometown of painter Dong Qichang. It's located in today's Songjiang in Shanghai), and the Zhe School (named after Zhejiang Province, home of painter Dai Jin. Artists of this school paid special attention to technique, and pursued varied styles).

An overwhelming majority of the members belonging to the above schools were important flower-and-bird painters, while the genre of landscape painting flourished simultaneously.

In addition, literati painting found its finest expression in the works of Dong Qichang, who was regarded as a paragon by his contemporaries in the late years of the Ming Dynasty.

Technically, the skill of *xie-yi* (freehand brushwork) in wash painting had attained to perfection. Both Xu Wei and Chen Chun were masters versed in *xie-yi* flower-and-bird painting. However, in contrast with *xie-yi*, Chen Hongshou created a new method of his own by using fine, delicate brush strokes and rich colors to vividly and accurately portray objects, so that achieving resemblance both in appearance and in spirit became possible.

Coupled with the development of the traditional landscape, literati and flower-and-bird painting was the renaissance of imperial-court decorative painting. There was a galaxy of artists in the imperial palace in those days, including Wang Fu, Lin Liang, Xu Yang, Guo Chun, Lü Ji, Ding Yunpeng and Bian Wenjin. They created a large number of imperishable works of art, which were handed down from generation to generation.

San You Bai Qin Tu('Three Friends' and 100 Birds)
Bian Wenjin
Ming Dynasty (1368—1644)
Color on silk
78.1 × 152.2cm

Bian Wenjin is a famous painter of the early Ming Dynasty skilled in fine-brushwork flower-and-bird painting. The dates of his birth and death are unknown. Carrying on the tradition of imperial-court decorative painting of the Southern Song Dynasty, he portrayed objects to a nicety in rich and gorgeous colors, and won the fame of top imperial painter of the Ming Dynasty. This picture scroll made in the 11th year of Emperor Yongle (1413) depicts the "three friends" of pine, bamboo and plum, which don't wither in winter, as well as 100 auspicious, very life-like birds in different shapes, and has been regarded as one of the painter's representative works.

Chun Hua San Xi (Spring Blossom and Three Magpies)
Bian Wenjin
Ming Dynasty (1368—1644)
Color on silk
165.2 × 98.3cm

The picture depicts two magpies fighting with each other on the ground, while a third one, watching the fight on a bamboo branch, seems to root for both sides. It has a rich flavor of imperial-court decorative painting of the Song Dynasty.

Hua Niao (Flowers and Birds)
Zhou Zhimian
Ming Dynasty (1368—1644)
Color on silk
87 × 36cm

Zhou Zhimian (ca. 1521—1600) is
a renowned flower-and-bird
painter of the Ming Dynasty
skilled in both fine-and freehand-
brushwork painting. This picture
made in the 16th year of Emperor
Wanli (1588) vividly portrays
egrets, hibiscus flowers, bees and
dragonflies, all different in shape.

雜卉爛春色環峯
積雨痕譬若古貞
士終身伴菜根
唐寅

Li Shi Cong Hui Tu (Upright Rocks and Flowers in Clusters)
Tang Yin
Ming Dynasty (1368–1644)
Ink and wash on paper
40 × 76cm

Tang Yin (1470–1523) of the Ming Dynasty is well-known for his landscape, figure and flower-and-bird paintings, and has a good command of calligraphy, painting, and poem and essay writing. One of the most outstanding painters in Chinese history, Tang who is noted for his refined and tasteful behavior claimed to be "South China's number one gallant young scholar." This picture scroll of rocks and flowers drawn in a succinct style is pregnant with meaning.

Shu Cai (Vegetable)
Shen Zhou
Ming Dynasty (1368–1644)
Ink and wash on paper
92.3 × 31.7cm

Shen Zhou (1427–1509) from Changzhou (the present Suzhou of Jiangsu Province) is a famous calligrapher and painter of the Ming Dynasty, good at drawing landscape in ink and wash and portraying flowers, birds and animals with freehand brushwork. Even a vegetable was worthy of the painter's brush and then became a priceless masterpiece. This is clear proof that the artist has attained the acme of perfection in painting.

宣闌百鳥羣閜哦
庭寒暑何似枝頸
鵙聲、能與雨

沈周

Jiu Sheng Huan Yu (Turtledove
Calling for Rain)
Shen Zhou
Ming Dynasty (1368—1644)
Ink and wash on paper
51.1 × 30.4cm

The artist portrays with simple,
light touches a turtledove sitting
on a budding branch and calling
for rain.

Shui Xian La Mei (Narcissuses and Wintersweet)
Qiu Ying
Ming Dynasty (1368−1644)
Color on silk
47.5 × 25cm

Qiu Ying (ca. 1502−1552) of the Ming Dynasty is expert in drawing figures, landscape, pavilions, flowers and birds. His painting is characterized by an exquisite, elegant style and bright, gorgeous colors.

Lan Zhu Tu (Orchid and Bamboo)
Wen Zhengming
Ming Dynasty (1368—1644)
Ink and wash on paper
40 × 76cm

In a simple but unconventional style, the painter creates an elegant, lofty artistic mood in this work of art.

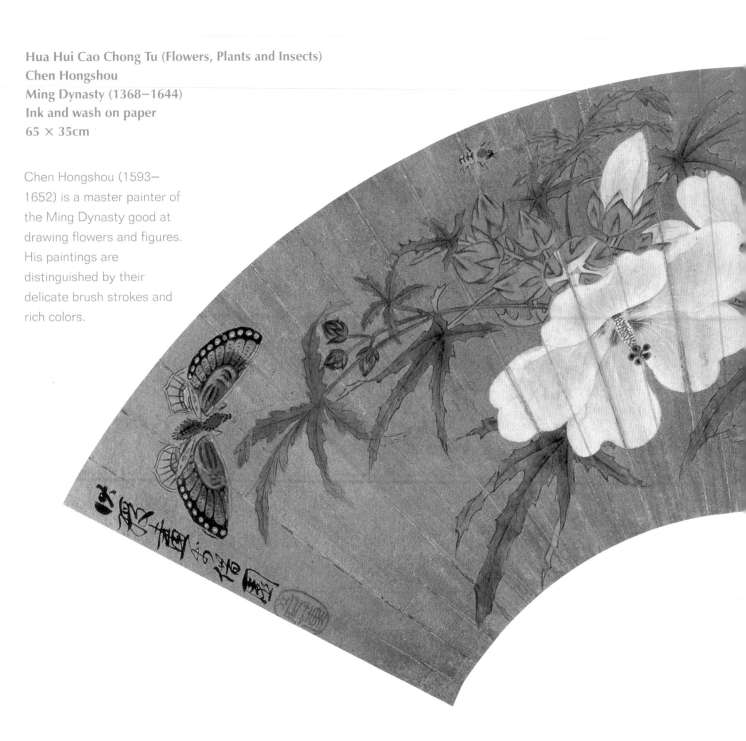

Hua Hui Cao Chong Tu (Flowers, Plants and Insects)
Chen Hongshou
Ming Dynasty (1368—1644)
Ink and wash on paper
65 × 35cm

Chen Hongshou (1593—1652) is a master painter of the Ming Dynasty good at drawing flowers and figures. His paintings are distinguished by their delicate brush strokes and rich colors.

She Se Hua Hui
(Colored Flowers)
Chen Chun
Ming Dynasty (1368—1644)
Color on paper
188 × 96.9cm

This is a masterpiece of Chen Chun (1493—1544) from Changzhou (the present Wuxian County of Jiangsu Province), who was famous for his refined brushwork and meticulous style even in his youth.

無苔書長葛中藥
花隆和筆在椒陵
白玉堂
謝隆

87

Qiu Lu Fu Rong (Autumn Egrets and Hibiscus)
Lü Ji
Ming Dynasty (1368–1644)
Color on silk
192.6 × 111.9cm

In this picture scroll a weeping willow, egrets, withered lotus leaves and hibiscus flowers make a beautiful autumn scene.

Song Niao Tu (Pine and Birds)
Wang Zhong
Ming Dynasty (1368–1644)
Color on silk
143 × 77cm

Wang Zhong's paintings are distinguished by a combination of *gong-bi* (fine brushwork) and *xie-yi* (freehand brushwork), bright colors, and well-balanced composition. The dates of his birth and death are unknown.

雲濤汪中戴墨

Xian He (Crane)
Zhang Pingshan
Ming Dynasty (1368—1644)
Color on silk
131 × 67cm

The original name of Zhang
Pingshan (1461—1537; or 1464—
1538) is Zhang Lu. He is skilled in
drawing figures, landscape, birds,
animals, and flowers.

Hua Niao Tu (A Flower-and-bird Painting)
Zhang Chong
Ming Dynasty (1368–1644)
Ink and wash on paper
65 × 35cm

Zhang Chong (1502–1579) from
Jiangning (the present Nanjing of
Jiangsu Province) is a well-known
painter of the Ming Dynasty, good
at drawing figures, birds and
flowers. This elegant flower-and-
bird sketch shows the hand of a
master.

Flower-and-bird Paintings of the Qing Dynasty

The Qing Dynasty (1616–1911) was another period of full bloom in terms of the creation of flower-and-bird paintings, which also experienced significant changes.

First of all, with the promotion and participation of successive emperors, the imperial-court decorative painting was all the rage at the time, leading to the emergence of a large number of imperial painters: Jiang Tingxi, Lang Shih-ning (or Giuseppe Castiglione), to name but a few. Jiang introduced the technique of Western painting and founded the "Jiang school of flower-and-bird painting," which had created a furor in the capital city of Beijing. Castiglione was an Italian painter who served in the Qing imperial palace. In front of his horse and flower-and-bird paintings, viewers can trace a good combination of Chinese and Western elements and find themselves in an entirely new world.

Secondly, following their Ming Dynasty predecessors, the literati painters in the early Qing Dynasty were bold in blazing new trails, and formed various schools of painting. Great masters of flower-and-bird painting included Wang Hui and Yun Shouping belonging to the school of "Four Wangs, Wu and Yun" (referring to the six famous painters, namely Wang Shimin, Wang Jian, Wang Hui, Wang Yuanqi, Wu Li and Yun Shouping. All favorites of the emperor, they were noted for their rigorous style. But there's no lack of wit and humor in their works); Shi Tao and Zhu Da of the "Four Monks" (referring to the four well-known monk painters, i.e. Shi Tao, Zhu Da, Shi Xi and Jian-Jiang. Living in the early years of the Qing Dynasty, they were well versed in poetry writing and calligraphy, and their paintings were distinguished by a powerful, free style. They were used to inscribing poems on their paintings to express personal opinions on the political situation of the time); Jin Nong, Huang Shen, Wang Shishen, Li Shan, Zheng Xie and Li Fangying of the "Eight Eccentrics of Yangzhou" (referring to the eight painters -- Zheng Xie, Luo Pin, Huang Shen, Li Fangying, Jin Nong, Li Shan, Wang Shishen, and Gao Xiang -- who sold their paintings in Yangzhou of Jiangsu Province in the period of Emperor Qianlong); as well as Hua Yan, Bian Shoumin and Gao Fenghan. Thanks to their efforts, the genre of literati painting had its heyday in the middle of the Qing Dynasty, and exerted a tremendous influence on the art circle. The plum flowers drawn by Jin Nong and the bamboos by Zheng Banqiao (Zheng Xie's literary name) have been widely commended even today.

In the middle and late Qing Dynasty, four painters -- Ren Xiong, Ren Xun, Ren Yi and Ren Yu -- came into prominence. They were also known as the "Four Rens." In particular, Ren Yi inherited the technique of *mo-gu* or "boneless" painting (drawing without outline but with forms achieved by washes of ink and color) from Yun Shouping, and made flower-and-bird painting attain a level never known before.

The following generation of flower-and-bird painters included Zhao Zhiqian, Xu-Gu and Wu Changshuo. In Wu Changshuo particularly all previous techniques of painting were synthesized and brought to their highest development. Wu whose life spanned the late Qing Dynasty and the Republic of China (1912−1949) was proficient in calligraphy, painting, poetry writing and seal engraving. He ushered in a new era of flower-and-bird painting.

Hua Hui (Flowers)
Yun Shouping
Qing Dynasty (1616−1911)
Color on silk
116.5 × 54.2cm

Yun Shouping (1633−1690) from Wujin (the present Changzhou of Jiangsu Province) is a renowned painter of the Qing Dynasty, good at drawing landscape and flowers. He has brought the technique of *mo-gu* or "boneless" painting to its highest development. Imitating painters of the Song Dynasty, he portrays in this picture an old tree, peony and magnolia flowers to symbolize wealth, magnificence and longevity. The scroll is distinguished by bright colors, excellent composition and delicate brushwork, giving viewers a sensation of pleasure.

Mo Gu Hua Hui Tu Ce
(An Imitation of An Ancient Flower Album-I)
Yun Shouping
Qing Dynasty (1616–1911)
Ink and wash on paper
26.2 × 33.3cm

Selected from the artist's album of flower paintings, this picture is characterized by its exquisite colors and unrestrained brush strokes.

Mo Gu Hua Hui Tu Ce (An Imitation of An Ancient Flower Album-II)
Yun Shouping
Qing Dynasty (1616–1911)
Ink and wash on paper
26.2 × 33.3cm

Mo Gu Hua Hui Tu Ce (An Imitation of An Ancient Flower Album-III)
Yun Shouping
Qing Dynasty (1616—1911)
Ink and wash on paper
58 × 40cm

**Ying Su Tu
(Poppy Flowers)
Liu Yu
Qing Dynasty (1616–
1911)
Color on silk
71.9 × 39.9cm**

Liu Yu from Wuxian
County (the present
Suzhou of Jiangsu
Province) is a famous
painter of the Qing
Dynasty, good at drawing
figures, landscape, trees,
mountain rocks, towers
and pavilions. The dates
of his birth and death are
unknown. This picture
made with delicate
brushwork had been kept
in the Qing imperial
palace.

Ju Hua Tu (Chrysanthemums)
Lang Shih-ning (Giuseppe Castiglione)
Qing Dynasty (1616—1911)
Color on silk
39.2 × 47cm

Lang Shih-ning (or Giuseppe Castiglione, 1688-1766), an Italian, served as an imperial painter during the Qing Dynasty. He came to China in the 54th year of Emperor Kangxi (1715), and then joined the Imperial Art Academy to begin his 50-year painting career in this country. A leading imperial painter in the period of Emperors Yongzheng and Qianlong, Castiglione successfully combined the technique of Western painting and traditional Chinese painting, and produced a great impact on the creation of imperial-court decorative paintings. A skilled portraitist as well as good at drawing figures, landscape, animals, flowers and birds, the artist is especially known for his horse paintings. This chrysanthemum picture is selected from his "Xian E Chang Chun Tu" ("Everlasting Verdure of the Immortal Calyx: An Album of Flower Studies").

Shao Yao Tu (Herbaceous Peony Flowers)
Lang Shih-ning (Giuseppe Castiglione)
Qing Dynasty (1616–1911)
Color on silk
39.2 × 47cm

This is selected from the artist's "Xian E Chang Chun Tu" ("Everlasting Verdure of the Immortal Calyx: An Album of Flower Studies").

Yu Mei Ren Hu Die Hua Tu (Corn Poppy and Fringed Iris)
Lang Shih-ning (Giuseppe Castiglione)
Qing Dynasty (1616–1911)
Color on silk
39.2 × 47cm

This is selected from the artist's "Xian E Chang Chun Tu" ("Everlasting Verdure of the Immortal Calyx: An Album of Flower Studies").

Gu Hua Ji Sui Tu (Millet Flowers and Spikes)
Lang Shih-ning (Giuseppe Castiglione)
Qing Dynasty (1616–1911)
Color on silk
39.2 × 47cm

This is selected from the artist's "Xian E Chang Chun Tu" ("Everlasting Verdure of the Immortal Calyx: An Album of Flower Studies").

Jin Chun Tu (Spring Pheasants)
Lang Shih-ning (Giuseppe Castiglione)
Qing Dynasty (1616–1911)
Color on silk
68.1 × 121.7cm

The artist portrays the pheasants with the technique of Western painting, while drawing the mountain rocks, streams and plants with the technique of traditional Chinese painting. This is thus a perfect combination of Chinese and Western elements with the overall tableau having a strong Chinese flavor.

**Wu Tong Shuang Tu (Phoenix Tree
and a Pair of Rabbits)**
Leng Mei
Qing Dynasty (1616–1911)
Color on silk
175.9 × 95cm

Leng Mei is an imperial painter of
the Qing Dynasty. The dates of
his birth and death are unknown.
A disciple of famous painter Jiao
Bingzhen, Leng is good at
drawing figures, beautiful women,
flowers and birds, and well-
known for his meticulous,
exquisite and decorative style.
Some Western elements can be
traced in this picture, which was
drawn with delicate brushwork
and distinguished by its rich
colors.

Mu Dan Shuang Shou Tu (Peony Flowers and a Pair of Paradise Flycatchers)
Yu Xing
Qing Dynasty (1616—1911)
Color on silk
174.4 × 97.6cm

Yu Xing (1692—1767) is an imperial painter of the Qing Dynasty. A disciple of flower-and-bird painter Jiang Tingxi, he is good at drawing flowers, birds, insects, fish, orchids, bamboos, narcissuses, and butterflies in particular. Sometimes using the technique of Western painting, the artist's style characterized by a fondness for bright colors is best embodied in this picture scroll.

Fu Rong Xi Shui Tu (Waterside Hibiscus Flowers)
Li Bingde
Qing Dynasty (1616–1911)
Color on paper
171.2 × 72.3cm

Li Bingde (1737–1807) from Wuxian County (the present Suzhou of Jiangsu Province) is an imperial painter of the Qing Dynasty. A disciple of painter Zhang Zongcang, he is good at drawing flowers, feathers, and landscape in rich, bright colors.

He Hua Tu (Lotus Flowers)
Li Bingde
Qing Dynasty (1616—1911)
Color on paper
136 × 101.5cm

In front of this sketch, viewers
seem to be able to smell the
scent of a lotus pond.

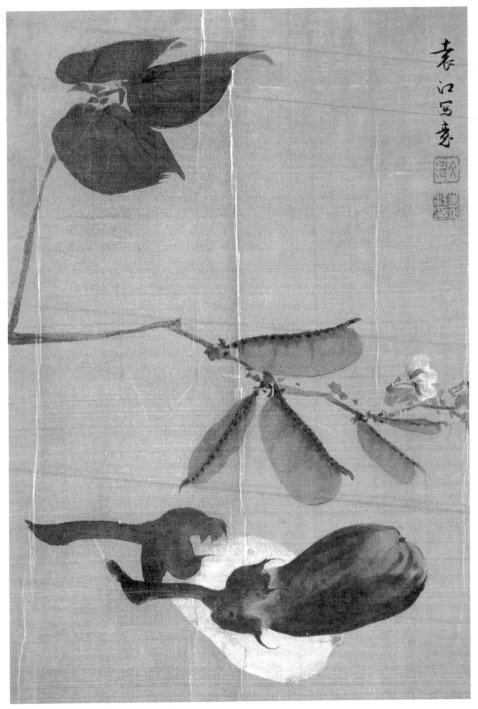

Xie Sheng Shu Guo Tu (A Sketch of Vegetables)
Yuan Jiang
Qing Dynasty (1616—1911)
Color on silk
22 × 32cm

Yuan Jiang (1671—1746) is a renowned imperial painter living in the period of Emperor Yongzheng (1678—1735). Known for his landscape, pavilion paintings and delicate, flowery style, he enjoyed the fame of "number 1 painter in the Qing Dynasty." Occasionally he drew flowers and birds. This sketch of eggplants and kidney beans is full of idyllic flavor.

**Xue Jiao Shuang He Tu
(Snow-clad Banana Tree
and a Pair of Cranes)
Yuan Yao
Qing Dynasty (1616-1911)
Color on silk
160 × 95cm**

Yuan Yao (?—ca. 1746),
nephew of Yuan Jiang, is
also an imperial painter of
the Qing Dynasty. Known
for his landscape and
pavilion paintings, he
occasionally drew flowers
and birds. This sketch
depicts a banana tree and
a pair of cranes standing in
snow, and gives viewers a
refreshing feeling.

He Hua Tu (Lotus Flowers)
Liu Shu
Qing Dynasty (1616–1911)
Color on silk
159.8 × 94.6cm

Liu Shu (1759–1816) is a painter living in the period of Emperors Qianlong and Jiaqing. He is good at drawing landscape, flowers and birds with elegant, fine brushwork. This sketch of a summer lotus pond is completed with the "boneless" technique (i. e. painting without outline but with forms achieved by washes of ink and color). The artist depicts with light ink some lotus flowers that "emerge unstained from the filth."

Yu Tang Fu Gui Tu (Wealth and Honor)
Yu Yuan
Qing Dynasty (1616–1911)
Color on silk
232.7 × 133.3cm

Yu Yuan is a flower-and-bird painter of the Qing Dynasty. The dates of his birth and death are unknown. He is skilled in imitating the ancients to draw flowers and feathers. This picture depicts a magnolia tree, peony flowers and peacocks with magnificent composition to symbolize riches and honor.

San Ba Tu (Offering Birthday Felicitations)
Zhao Zhiqian
Qing Dynasty (1616–1911)
Color on silk
165 × 66cm

Zhao Zhiqian (1829–1884) is a famous calligrapher, painter and seal cutter in the late years of the Qing Dynasty. Especially good at drawing flowers, vegetables and fruits with freehand brushwork, he is well-known for his figure, landscape and flower-and-bird paintings. Following the examples of Xu Wei, Zhu Da as well as the "Eight Eccentrics of Yangzhou," he painted with great ease and powerful strokes. An important painter of the so-called "Shanghai School," he initiated a unique style of drawing flowers with freehand brushwork in rich, bright colors, to suit both refined and popular tastes. His style has had great influence on the painting of later ages.

Song He Yan Nian (Pine Tree and Cranes for Longevity)
Li Shan
Qing Dynasty (1616–1911)
Color on paper
173 × 91cm

Li Shan (1686–1760) is a renowned painter of the Qing Dynasty. Once an imperial painter, he later resigned and returned to Yangzhou to make a living by selling his paintings. He is skilled in drawing landscape, flowers and birds with freehand brushwork, and has produced a great impact on the painting of later ages. This work of art has the rich flavor of literati painting, demonstrating that by then the artist had completely got rid of the tradition of imperial-court decorative painting and formed a style of his own.

項易庵

蘭之生深林止以娟幽獨采作立
中供人之眼鼻福胡為乎而人把
玩珠不漬三亜生豪瑞經管機在目
展卷六七花鮮亲不恋簡神物
自通靈碩之如育馥誰欲近代華
我為思鼎足簡劫陳句賜輕窒
平卅
家孫

**Hua Hui Tu Ce (Album of
Flowers-I)**
Xiang Shengmo
Qing Dynasty (1616—1911)
Color on paper
31 × 23.8cm

Xiang Shengmo (1597—
1658) is from Xiushui (the
present Jiaxing of Zhejiang
Province). Selected from
his album of flowers, this
picture depicts orchids with
accurate, lively brush
strokes and rich colors,
fully demonstrating the
artist's unique style.

當聞半面妝
又覿觀音變
奇兮靡定姿
忽二竅人炫
家珍

周卿銅雀春何處秋圃年二鎖
二高只問澹粧濃抹意為誰啼
笑兩般嬌 一項晉禛詩畫

Hua Hui Tu Ce
(Album of Flowers-II)
Xiang Shengmo
Qing Dynasty (1616—1911)
Color on paper
31 × 23.8cm

Hua Hui Tu (Flowers-I)
Zhao Zhiqian
Qing Dynasty (1616—1911)
Color on paper
22.4 × 31.5cm

Zhao Zhiqian (1829—1884) from Kuaiji (the present Shaoxing of Zhejiang Province) is a famous painter of the Qing Dynasty. He is also expert in calligraphy and seal cutting. He draws flowers in rich, bright colors, producing a similar effect to that of the Western painting.

Hua Hui Tu (Flowers-II)
Zhao Zhiqian
Qing Dynasty (1616–1911)
Color on paper
22.4 × 31.5cm

坐雲中秋月正圓玲
瓏丹桂植當天臺私著
照八荒外皎潔濤光雲
瀋逢 中秋望月

Gui Hua (Sweet-scented Osmanthus)
Jiang Tingxi
Qing Dynasty (1616-1911)
Color on silk
172.8 × 74.5cm

Court painter Jiang Tingxi (1669-
1732), styled Nansha and Yangsun,
was also known by his literary names
of Xigu and Retired Scholar
Qingtong. Jiang from Changshu,
Jiangsu Province served as the
Great Scholar in the Qing Dynasty.
His flower-and-bird paintings made in
the so-called "Jiang Style" are art
treasures. His extant works include
"Bamboos and Rocks," "Flowers,"
"Mother Chrysanthemums" and "Four
Mascots Celebrating Harvest."
Inscriptions by Emperor Kangxi add
value to this picture drawn in elegant
colors and delicate strokes.

Hua Guo Tu (Flowers and Fruits-I)
Zhou Xian
Qing Dynasty (1616–1911)
Color on paper
28.6 × 28cm

Zhou Xian (1820–1875) from Xiushui (the present Jiaxing of Zhejiang Province) is a painter of the late Qing Dynasty, who is good at drawing flowers. This sketch of gourds shows the artist's style characterized by a combination of freehand and delicate brushwork, which is reminiscent of painter Ren Xiong's.

Hua Guo Tu (Flowers and Fruits-II)
Zhou Xian
Qing Dynasty (1616–1911)
Color on paper
28.6 × 28cm

This sketch of vegetables drawn with freehand brushwork is distinguished by a strong idyllic flavor.

Hua Hui (Flowers)
Wang Wu
Qing Dynasty (1616–1911)
Color on silk
104 × 38cm

Living in the early Qing Dynasty,
Wang Wu (1632–1690) is an
imperial painter noted for his
flower-and-bird paintings.
Imitating the artists of the Song
and Yuan dynasties, he formed a
style of his own characterized by
a combination of delicate and
freehand brushwork.

Hua Niao (Flowers and Birds)
Wang Wu
Qing Dynasty (1616–1911)
Color on paper
127.5 × 35cm

This flower-and-bird painting is
full of royal grandeur.

Ju (Chrysanthemums)
Yun Bing
Qing Dynasty (1616−1911)
Color on paper
89 × 33cm

The dates of the painter's birth and death are unknown. This chrysanthemum scroll is drawn with meticulous, exquisite brush strokes.

Hua Hui (Flowers)
Cixi
Qing Dynasty (1616–1911)
Color on paper
125.5 × 65cm

Cixi (1835–1908) was the highest-
ranking concubine of Emperor
Xianfeng, and held court from behind
a screen (an empress regent was
supposed to be concealed from the
sight of ministers at audience) for
over 40 years during the period of
Emperors Tongzhi and Guangxu. It is
said that Cixi was fond of calligraphy
and painting in her later years, and
often awarded her works that were
mostly made by others to her
ministers. This picture of peony
flowers is highly decorative. The
flowerpot and stand of excellent
workmanship are apparently products
of a government porcelain kiln.

Shu Guo (Vegetables and Fruits)
Lu Hui
Qing Dynasty (1616–1911)
Color on silk
330 × 33cm

Lu Hui (1851–1920) is an important painter of the "Shanghai School" in the late Qing Dynasty. He is good at drawing landscape, figures, flowers, birds, vegetables and fruits. This picture depicting pomegranates, peaches and fingered citrons is a typical birthday gift in ancient China.

Qiu Hua Qi Shi Tu (Autumn Flowers and Rock)
Shen Shijie
Qing Dynasty (1616–1911)
Color on paper
70.8 × 79.2cm .

Shen Shijie (living in the latter half of the 19th century) is an imperial painter in the period of Emperor Tongzhi. He is noted for his figure and flower paintings. This picture is distinguished by its delicate brushwork and ingenious composition.

Hua Niao Tu (Flowers and Birds-I)
Ren Xun
Qing Dynasty (1616–1911)
Color on paper
26.2 × 35.7cm

Ren Xun (1835–1893) from Xiaoshan of Zhejiang Province is good at drawing figures, flowers and feathers. Ren Xun, Ren Xiong, Ren Yi and Ren Yu were jointly called the "Four Rens." The artist portrays sprays of blossoms with "boneless" technique (painting without outline but with forms achieved by washes of ink and color). A flying swallow adds vitality to the originally still tableau. The composition is really ingenious.

Hua Niao Tu (Flowers and Birds-II)
Ren Xun
Qing Dynasty (1616–1911)
Color on paper
26.2 × 35.7cm

The picture vividly depicts a bird resting on a branch.

**Hua Niao Tu
(Flowers and Birds-I)
Ren Yi
Qing Dynasty (1616—1911)
Color on silk
160 × 58.5cm**

Ren Yi (1840—1896) from Shanyin
(the present Shaoxing of Zhejiang
Province) is good at drawing
figures, landscape, flowers and
birds. In his youth he already
enjoyed fleeting fame. Learning the
technique of Western painting, he
formed a vigorous and free style of
his own.

Hua Niao Tu
(Flowers and Birds-II)
Ren Yi
Qing Dynasty (1616—1911)
Color on silk
160 × 58.5cm

Compared with the previous one,
the composition of this picture is
more ingenious and unconventional.

Hua Hui (Flowers)
Ma Jiatong
Qing Dynasty (1616–1911)
Color on silk
33.5 × 173cm

Ma Jiatong is a famous flower-and-bird painter. The dates of his birth and death are unknown. Noted for his landscape and flower-and-bird paintings, sometimes he also drew figure or Buddha portraits. Mostly he drew plants and birds with both delicate and freehand brushwork.

名園芍藥見重臺
正是西月維夏寿の海
去駐隨緣室昌碩筆七年六

Shu Hua He Bi Tu
(A Combination of Calligraphy and Painting-I)
Wu Changshuo
Qing Dynasty (1616—1911)
Color on paper
33 × 37cm

Wu Changshuo (1844—1927) is a well-known poet, calligrapher and seal cutter as well as a flower-and-bird master painter in modern times. In Wu all previous techniques of the literati painting are synthesized and brought to their highest development. This painting of herbaceous peony drawn by freehand brushwork, with the artist's inscriptions on it, fully demonstrates Wu's artistic attainments.

Shu Hua He Bi Tu
(A Combination of Calligraphy and Painting-II)
Wu Changshuo
Qing Dynasty (1616–1911)
Color on paper
33 × 37cm

The peony painting drawn with freehand brushwork, and the cited verses depicting Lady Yang of the Tang Dynasty, bring out the best in each other.

图书在版编目（CIP）数据

中国历代花鸟画：英文／李向平主编；邵达译.—北京：五洲传播出版社，2007.8
ISBN 978-7-5085-1128-3

Ⅰ.中...　Ⅱ.①李...　②邵...　Ⅲ.花鸟画－作品集－中国　Ⅳ.J222
中国版本图书馆 CIP 数据核字（2007）第 092266 号
Flower-and-Bird Painting in Ancient China
Editor in chief: Li Xiangping
Translator: Shao Da
Published and distributed by China Intercontinental Press in August 2007
ISBN 978-7-5085-1128-3

中国历代花鸟画

主　　编：李向平
副 主 编：林武汉
统筹策划：荆孝敏
撰　　稿：刘奉文
图片编辑：蔡　程
装祯设计：仁　泉
翻　　译：邵　达
责任编辑：荆孝敏　　王莉
设计承制：北京紫航文化艺术有限公司
印　　刷：北京盛天行健印刷有限公司
Flower-and-Bird Painting in Ancient China
Editor in chief: Li Xiangping
Associate editor in chief: Lin Wuhan
Overall planner: Jing Xiaomin

Writer: Liu Fengwen

Picture editor: Cai Cheng

Page layout design: Ren Quan

Translator: Shao Da

Executive editors: Jing Xiaomin, Wang Li

Binding and layout undertaken by Beijing Zihang Culture & Art Co., Ltd.

Printed by Beijing Amstrong Printing Co., Ltd.

出版发行：五洲传播出版社

地址：中国北京市海淀区北小马厂 6 号　　邮编：100038

发行电话：010-58891281　　　网址：www.cicc.org.cn

Published and distributed by China Intercontinental Press

No.6 Beixiaomachang, Haidian District, Beijing, China

Post code: 100038

Telephone: 010-58891281

Website: www.cicc.org.cn

开本：210 × 210　1/20　　印张：10

2007 年 8 月第 1 版　2009 年 10 月第 2 次印刷

ISBN 978-7-5085-1128-3

定价：146.00 元

Format: 210 × 210　1/20

Printed sheets: 10

First edition in August 2007, Second Printing in October 2009

ISBN 978-7-5085-1128-3

Price: ¥146.00(RMB)